INCUBATION A SPACE FOR MONSTERS

LEON WORKS

BHANU KAPIL

INCUB

ATION

A Space for Monsters

Copyright © 2006 by Bhanu Kapil

ISBN 978-0-9765820-2-1

Design and composition by Quemadura

Leon Works logo by Caitlin Parker

Printed on acid-free, recycled paper

LEON WORKS: Providence

THIRD PRINTING, 2011

FOR MELISSA BUZZEO

CONTENTS

Organisms emerge from a discursive process. Biology is a discourse, not the living world itself. But humans are not the only actors in the construction of the entities of any scientific discourse; machines (delegates that can produce surprises) and other partners (not "pre- or extra-discursive objects," but partners) are active constructors of natural scientific objects. Like other scientific bodies, organisms are not ideological constructions. The whole point about discursive construction has been that it is not about ideology. Always radically historically specific, always lively, bodies have a different kind of specificity and effectivity; and so they invite a different kind of engagement and intervention.

DONNA HARAWAY

The Promises of Monsters:
A Regenerative Politics for
Inappropriate/d Others

HANDWRITTEN

PREFACE

TO REVERSE

THE BOOK

AND

NOTES ON

MONSTERS

(1-3)

1 Reverse the book in duration. What does that mean? I am writing to you. These notes now when it's too late.

2 If the cyborg you read about in bookstores is an immigrant from Mexico crossing into the U.S. beneath a floodlit court, then mine is a Punjabi-British hitchhiker on a JI visa. This is tunneling as seen from a satellite—a sort of concave warp in the dirt of the line.

3 She lives in a house with others, including animals, creating individual spaces of companionship and ardor. What happens when this domestic life grows suspect? When the glass reverts in its granular drag to the subject of architecture: the failure of a house to believe in its occupants?

4 Mate with surfaces. Okay. Hitchhike. Okay. Make a cup of Darjeeling tea and start walking down a sidewalk in America. I saw this in a film starring George Clooney; no, Natalie Wood. The last scene is her, the gamine self, kicking off her shoes as the house explodes behind her. Perpetrating, she doesn't flinch. Sips tea. Keeps walking. I wanted to write that. Continuance. As it related to loss. The secret pleasure of refusing to live like a normal person in a dress/with a sex drive and fingers/dreamy yet stabilized in the café of languages.

5   I want to have sex with what I want to become. This is a statement related to women arriving in a country it would be regressive to leave. Then, writing, I was filled with a longing for —for what? George-in-the-flesh? George Clooney in Idaho, pretending to pick up hitchhikers as research for his next movie in which he plays a mild-mannered serial killer? No. A different series of acts. Tricky. For example, I'm embarrassed by this book. It makes my blood roar to think of you reading it. So intimate. A text. Then it is a document related to shame flooding the body to make it red. Who doesn't want to heal a human body? Who doesn't want a perfect human body? The body of my hitchhiker is, thus, inevitably female or Punjabi, fused to the production of secrets. There are no e-mails home from the e-mail café. Nothing. Phone calls, bullshitting. Sickening. I mean, what is this girl/my girl doing, there in a foreign heartland like a dog with a thumb? My Laloo, about to do it. Don't do it, little one. Red dress. Don't get into the car.

6   But then, lit up, a red wife, kind of, not really, she sets out to see things as they are. Describes a virtual countryside. Jumps a box car. Drinks domestic beer. Okay. She does it and I write it down: a damaged eye with votive filaments. (I am writing to you.) "No point in writing home." Then what?

4

PRE (1)

1 Here in the house. Dear Laloo, I painted my door yellow today and pinned up a picture of a woman facing a red wall, her palms dragging the red down. Is it you? Is it blood? She's wearing cords because it's 1978 and she's painting, somewhere in Iowa.

2 Covering the scrap of paper with layers of selloptape. I mean, sticky tape, like cell function: the central space surrounded or wrapped in a transparent life-like membrane. I was writing about you (Laloo) then sticking it up there, on the door above the woman, in the most beautiful house in the world. Taping it up, like a damaged leg or knee. You're my damage girl today.

3 It's not the same when I just write it out in my notebook. I like the paper separately. Visually, a series. Then I can say to visitors: what comes next for a red girl? They don't care. They just want the tea or coffee and are happy to exchange elaborate stories of girlhood. Exhausted, we lean our heads on the kitchen table in turn, sucking on a piece of chocolate or black Panda licorice, listening to the obvious words at the end of a girl. What a girl is. Sometimes you are fifteen years old in the stories I tell. Sometimes you are not the red of technology but monstrous or infrared, visible through the walls of a house.

4   Okay. Monsters. No, I need my notebook. Okay, here it is: "If cyborgs." If cyborgs are smooth, then Laloo ... Is she? Are you? I don't know what that means, the biological definition of a cyborg, except that I have to decide who you are, little pink/ fluorescing shrimp, little Laloo, before I write you out of the sea and onto the shore. Pre-text. Reversed. Perhaps it's just the imperfection of the altering surgery that makes you seem, to the untrained eye, a little stilted. Prehensile. Or if this is, in a community, something even lovers/customers or host families could adapt to. Your redness and lack of language. Small amounts of loss. Is it your real blood that makes you so richly you, Laloo? Is it the fake blood they have in the prop department, in vials? I dress you in red or paint you red, overlaying your delicate form with the scarlet form of charcoal, a blunt, creamy pastel crayon.

5   I place my hand in yours, though you have no sensation there, where I extend support to you. When I describe you, deep in the story with its delicious hospital and unpredictable patients, you feel it everywhere in your body—the helping hand of the driver hauling you up into his four-wheeler, somewhere in Illinois or Maryland—and, in a spectral sense, so do I in my own body. I feel it (your grip) and adapt, immediately, to the trope or infidelity of the story I am telling. Your real hand inside the prosthesis inside the glove.

ı But I was thinking today about our conversation earlier in the summer. Exhausted, you lay your head on the kitchen table and said: "But what's the difference between a monster and a cyborg? I need something to eat. Do you have any chocolate?" Opening the fridge, I said quietly and perhaps too seriously, trying to impress you: "The monster is that being who refuses to adapt to her circumstances." Her fate. Her body. Great Britain. You said: "So, is Laloo English or British?" I said: "She's from London." But the more I said London, the more it sounded like a joke. LondonLondonLondon.

2 I was thinking today about what happens when you keep going in a car. This is something you can only do here. Wish for something. Did you ever do it? Wish you weren't there? I want that *go on, go* even though it is unclear to me what happens when you get to the Panama Canal or Idaho. Hitchhiking in Idaho as a veritable child, I was taken in by a farming couple, Fatty and Daddy, a hundred miles or so outside of Boise. Fatty was rail thin, about seventy-five, and Daddy was a big man who had a reclining chair in each room and looked younger than his wife. They picked me up in their truck—I was sitting by the side of the road, brushing the knots out of my hair with my fingers—and I stayed with them for five days. They said it was not the right thing for me to be in the open like that, and they took me to eat every day

at a restaurant called Country Buffet. In my innocence, I had been walking on a road that led to the country compound of a KKK leader/operative, Charles Reynold. What is an operative? It is someone who is always planning a way in, like the hen-house fox with his beautifully red, bushy tail. Daddy, Fatty, and I hunkered down until Daddy's nephew, Robert, stopped by on his way through nowhere and gave me a ride to Boise proper, where there was a bus station. I waited until Robert had gone and then I walked out to the main drag to get a cup of coffee and interview murderers. "I can take you as far as the state line." "That would be lovely." Obsessed, far from home with its gooseberry patches and grim professions based upon openings at Heathrow Airport or Nestle, the main employers in the dingy part of northwest London that constituted my origins, I said yes. Soft yes to the color green, which is going.

3   That is a tree (going) but also an ocean: a way of being saturated with color that only happens here in your country for me; for you it might happen in another place. Mine. Like Laloo, I lived for many years on an island with congested traffic flows. Thus, a juniper tree flying by the window, intensely blue, or the Atlantic Ocean, to the left, if the car has a destination to the south, such as to The Keys, is magical to me. Improbable in light of my origins. Hers. The girl in the car. I don't know. I am writing to you, in your special writing dress made from scraps of lace as if it (the dress, the morning of writing ahead of you) is a café; as if, writing, you

are hypnotizing not only the biologies of strangers and friends but also yourself. For this reason, when I think of you reading, I think of you as writing blindly. You read but you are also writing. As if my own eyes were closed, I see your white books floating in the sky above my painting of the red girl. These books are separate from my own work, here in the salt-water notebook, but they communicate with it in a nonlocal sense. Like birds.

4   This is pre but the notebook is after. Soaked already at the edge and foamy. Past future. Writing on warp when dry. Pages. Entries by hand. That is the morning I woke up and walked to the Pacific Ocean, after a night in a motel in Florence, Oregon, complete with a dodgy door and the reality of pillows. The woman at the front desk was wearing a very pretty apron with purple and yellow flowers on it. An expatriate, she said exaggeratedly, oblivious to our common origin: "About four miles. You're not going to walk, are you? Do you have an umbrella? You can't go out like that, ducky."

5   I walked towards the sound of something roaring in a day, the kind of day that is like darkness but lit up, on its forested, proximal verge by gorse, which is a bright yellow flower. Citron-yellow and a kind of tin or silver roofing with holes in it. The day. Like walking in a dreamed landscape drenched with the wrong rain. Monsoon. What kind of rain is this? I recognized the immensity but not the temperature. This was monstrous: the inability to assimilate, on the level of the senses, an ordinary expe-

rience of weather. Here is the tongue, for example, constantly darting out to feel the air: what is it? Is it summer? Is it a different season? It's a different day. That's okay. Damaged from her travels, in some sense unsettled, enormously anxious, a girl does it anyway: gets up and goes. It's as if the day has a memory of her and not the other way around.

HALLUCINATING CHILDHOOD (3)

ı "A monster hallucinates; a cyborg has a more sexual agenda. It is sexual to mate with surfaces. It is sexual to write in the café like an émigré." Oh, shut your face. It is something else to gag. It is something else to leave in a bad, magical way. The removal of a person, abruptly, from a set of conditions is complicated for the soul. Did you ever feel that? You, not Laloo. I am writing to you, a writer. As a child, in the space before writing, did you suffer when you went to other people's houses? Did you feel their homes to be superior to your own with its backward-seeming margarines and vinegars for preserving then cooking vegetables and animals? Were you born a cyborg into a house of brutal monsters who bickered over everything from feeding to sleeping schedules? Or did you, as the years passed, have the growing sense that you were a citizen born to immigrants? For example, could I ask if it ever seemed to you that, in the hospital, you had been taken from the wrong incubator by an exhausted, starving nurse twenty-one hours into a forty-eight hour shift? There is something about a monster that is formulated in these hours or days just after birth; a crossed or normal birth that, either way, is connected to a profound confusion deep in the routines of transference. The nurse transfers you from the arms of your birth parent to a basin to a kind of rectangular, high-wired dish. This is the incubator where hands in purple latex gloves massage you through a flexible, transparent wall, encouraging the circulation in your limbs. Gradually, you pink up, because all touch is good, even for Laloo, who went home with cyborgs. "Is Laloo a cyborg or is she a monster?" Laloo means red. It is a Punjabi nickname of the sort given to children and abandoned, in most cases, when the child is grown, sprouting hair and dripping blood all over the white, 1970s shag carpeting that extends diabolically into the bathroom and even the kitchen.

2 Pre-life: a wavering image on the screen like a comma in the hospital. Cars extend that pre. A monster gets in the car in the parking lot then gets out to wait for the next one, breaking it down for herself. The human action. Like a sentence. Very bad. Like a girl, she is coming into feeling and so the numbness she has in cars is both an obstacle to love, whether that is the love of a person or of one's country, and a boon. Like a coat. Here I am speaking of hitchhiking, which is the future. How a girl keeps going, far from buttered toast for breakfast and freezing rain lit from within by amber streetlights on winter mornings. That switching com-

bination of indigo and yellow she looks for wherever she goes. Asters and goldenrod along the highways of upstate New York. "Look it." Or what?

3 Like umbrellas with their alternating, elongated triangles of color. "Here." Fatty handed me a hundred-dollar bill as Daddy and Robert were fussing with the truck, strapping my suitcase on the bed with orange cables. Slipped it out of her apron with the sweetest smile I ever saw. I loved her. I loved them. Technically, at the age of twenty, I was not an adult female yet. Adults drink beer to excess, with lemon wedges in it. Robert was a bit boring, but I loved him too. Patsy Cline on the radio, which you never got, in the pre-pre, which was England.

4 I am writing to you because it is private and separate, like thinking.

5 "Cyborgs are built for assimilation into households and factories." Am I boring you? Do you want some coffee? "You adapt to them and they learn how to ask questions, verifying your answers before responding further. In horror films, you can't always tell if it is a cyborg or if it is a person, whereas monsters are always identifiable as such by their long black hair and multiple arms, retracted into the torso during lovemaking and hitchhiking, because even monsters fall in love, want to make a go of it. Endless reproduction is boring." The milk's in the fridge. I wrote ten Laloos, then killed them down.

6 My friend, it's 12:06 p.m. I have to stop writing now and go

to work. Writing is thinking. I don't like to think of you hitch-hiking because you are such a vulnerable figure in your Edwardian outfits. Please tell me my future. Your vulnerability as a writer makes you so open to astral images, the ones refracted from that other place. Reading palms or in your practice of hypnosis, an industry that supports your writing in an economic sense, do you ever frame these integrative images as destinies? I switch off when I hear the word destiny. Dear friend, where did I go? Where am I going? When you read my palm, it's as if you are hypnotizing my biology. Does a reader hypnotize a writer as much as the other way, the normal way, around? That is separate. Tell me. What made it possible for me to live in a township? Will I touch and be touched at the ten points of momentary clarity in the day, one for each waking hour, like the others in their housing units? These are questions I have had since childhood. "Shut your stupid face before I shut it for you."

7 An image from childhood for Laloo: I see a body, outlined against the barracks, coming down towards the beach. Her gestures are slowed-down, full of streaming whites. With precision and infinite gentleness, she places a red tongue into the foam. Red kelp dried in the sun higher up on the beach. This is a tongue she is holding in her hands, separate from her mouth. A seal curves its neck to look at her and then stays, its dark head bobbing in place. They stare at each other in the moonlight, which is the pre-animal space with no technology as yet for communicating be-

tween worlds. No exchange of fluids or bodies at the center of text. Nothing. No delicious hospital with its complex routines of health, of bringing people back from the edge of something.

⊟ A monster refuses her life and that is why I can only write to you. You were the one who said, on your last visit, over a plate of almond biscotti and Assam tea: "The more you refuse life, the more you write. This is writing." I tore that piece of paper and sellotaped it to my front door, next to the photograph of the woman streaming reds, the image of obeisance she offers to casual visitors.

⊟ Here in the childhood, at the limit of the house, what is she doing? I see her stepping out of her body and I don't like that at all. Her skin. Her skin was perfect and now it's all stretched out. Silver marks on brown skin, like a pregnancy. I could not stop her from giving birth to herself if I tried. Sometimes she leaves and does not come back, slamming the door. Sometimes she conceals a pregnancy, though she's nine years old. Sometimes she is real and they take her to the hospital against her wishes when she complains of a terrible stomachache.

10 A monster refuses to wait for the midwife, the surgeon, her mother, interns, or the Nigerian nurse, Fidelia Chimara, who has a needle and believes in Jesus with his company of angels. The needle is left, drooling, onto the white sheet; the nurse returns with bandages to find an empty hospital bed, which she re-fills, in moments, with a brief EH to an orderly. I know what the

nurse's name is because she told me when she brought me some tea from the machine. Exhausted, I was waiting forever.

11 Here: "I came into the rushing softness intact. Then I was not what I was in those first broken days with their sorries. Sorry, sorry, sorry, sorry, sorry, please forgive me." You wrote those words to me a long time ago and I kept them as an emblem of someone's effort to return to life regardless of their skills. I stuck them on the door. Those from you. You are my human contact. From the snowfields marked with copper circles, as seen from above: I write to you, a kind of discourse, in my notebook. Are you a woman? Were you a girl? I forgive you. Look, I am writing these notes to you on JetBlue, flying east over the heart of your country. If you are white, then were you pink, back then, in your childhood? Is pink a preliminary shade of red? Are you a red wife? I'm sorry. It doesn't sound right. Please forgive me.

12 No. Progress the biology. What is a streaming girl? "A monster refuses childhood with its berries and goes." A go is what you have. In this scene, a childhood or Christmas scene with its reds and greens against a white background, the girl says no to the local festival. As the adults feast upon lavish displays of tandoori chicken and deep-fried bread, she slips out into the real England. There, though she is very young, nine maybe, or ten, already menstruating yet dressed in a sequined, little girl's salwar-chemise, she gets in her dad's Ford Cortina and pulls the clutch. The car gags then coughs then goes. Because of the wet snow, nobody no-

tices, not even the police, when she drives to the end of the street then takes a left. By the time she reaches Dover with its scone and jam emporiums and holding centers complete with Iraqi and French interpreters, she's exhausted. She's no longer what a person could call a girl or even British. Mistakenly, she's detained. "Cat got your tongue, love?" After a few weeks, they ship her across the Channel on a train, which makes her panic, think about going home and saying, "Sorry, I said I'm sorry, I'll never do it again," but it's too late. In this sense, in silence and a sort of intense confusion, she takes revenge upon the idea of childhood, with its inescapable structures and customs, and escapes.

13 I said, "What is a monster?" You said: "Anybody different." I thought that was so amazing and I wrote it down in my notebook, in which I have been writing to you. Tearing out the pages as I go.

NOTES

AGAINST

A CYBORG

PREFACE

"Fig. 57-Laloo." In the encyclopedia of rare and extraordinary cases, *Anomalies and Curiosities of Medicine*, first published in 1896, I came upon this figure. I gave its name to her, my cyborg, when I read these words: "Quite recently there was exhibited in the museums of the United States an individual bearing the name "Laloo," who was born in Oudh, India, and was the second of four children." An anomaly, Laloo's chest was appended by a parasite, "which had its own intestinal tract." Two legs hung from him. Am I saying this well? He was duplicate, in a limited sense, within himself. Then I heard these words inside my own body: "He's a monster." Like a person in a dream, he was a concentrated block of wrong perceptions. Of late, disconcertingly, I've been dreaming of Laloo-like, Himalayan beings with multiple arms, heads, legs, and eyes. When I was a child, my mother blew warm air onto my closed eyelids, her lips pressing against the thin, un-real skin through a corner of the cotton, marigold-yellow sari she favored for kitchen work. It had a dark green, silver, and black border made of heavier material and inexpertly stitched to the soft yellow. Her skin smelled of pears from the cheap body lotion she bought every six months or so from the Wavy Line Market on

Lansbury Drive. In Punjabi, as I nestled against her in bed, she told me stories of complex deities: Shiva, Parvati, Hanuman, Durga. Each night, I asked for birds mixed with men and got them. I got ten thousand heads and eight arms, each reaching out for a different thing from the same body: conches, bloody swords, and pencils. I said, "Is that an angel, Mummy?" And she hit me, because we were Hindus and angels are Islamic. But what is an angel in retrospect? Whether red or white, it is a man in a dress with a different gender. It is a channel for information in the vertical sense. As a Baroque figure, an angel functions as an extension of the Renaissance babies on ceilings in Europe, where I was born and brought up in a disturbed way by parents whose hearts had broken in another civilization. (Collect the blood in a shallow bowl. Mix it with white feathers. Make a Laloo with twigs for the arms and a stick for the leg, then prop it up against the overgrown roots of a tree in your back garden.)

LALOO IS A BABY

A "laloo" is a kind of tin or bronze baby sold throughout West Bengal, in conjunction with a variety of outfits such as lemon-yellow and pink dresses that are pulled over the head of the baby laloo and settled on its hips and may be purchased separately. My mother said a laloo is the word Bengalis have for the baby Krishna and that they make offerings of milk and butter to the statue each morning, which is commonly (the laloo) placed on a shrine in the kitchen. Its dress is changed daily. I said, great. That's just fabulous. You gave me a boy's name. (As a child visiting India, I seemed very white and pink in my complexion, initially, and was called Laloo by the people in my family even when I darkened in the sun.) I said, Mummy, bloody hell, it's like being a girl with blonde hair and a skateboard who falls in love on the outskirts of Chicago, in a SUBURB, and has to say the following words to the cute boy who wants to kiss her: "My name is Jesus." My mother said, where's Chicago? What boy? Boys! Kissing! (And spat on the ground for emphasis, just to think of it, the exchange of germs plus the two open mouths.)

LALOO IS A CYBORG

"Who cyborgs will be is a matter of survival." Does she mean what they will be when they grow up? "I want to be a doctor." "I want to write opposites." Does she mean like that? I begin the night of writing in the orange alcove of my semi-rural U.S. home with the basic biological question above me like a faucet. If I turn it on, will it produce a warm solution? Should I screw a lightbulb into the faucet and make it red, the lightbulb, a throwback to 1960s mating rituals of the sort that made me? Like a cyborg who is responsible for basic chores, I choose a basic word deep inside what I want, which is the body, and begin there: a constant contact with a color. Red. She is thirsty. My cyborg. Her arms ache from holding her legs up. Which legs? Luxurious pubes but no opening. I read this in the dictionary of monsters in which they call the excess limbs, which are duplications of the lower extremities, parasitical. More notes on Fig. 57-Laloo: "The penis of the parasite was said to show signs of erection, at times, and urine passed through it without the boy's knowledge. Perspiration and elevation of temperature seemed to occur simultaneously in both. To pander to the morbid curiosity of the curious, the "Dime Museum" managers at one time shrewdly clothed the parasite in female attire, calling the two brother and sister; but there is no doubt that all the traces of sex were of the male type."

PRE-SYNTHETIC LALOO

Monsters who want something else. They want the pre and fix it. This is pre-synthesis: a human form constructed from a dermoid cyst but with memory. The body hangs its memory on itself, which is cystic, apparent, lolling. What is? Protuberance? An excess site or something, more accurately, that does not stay inside the central cavity with the other soft, breaded parts rich with blood vessels. This is blood text and I wrote it, tried to, in the alcove like a balcony next to the kitchen, asking my guests to help themselves to food and drink like family members. "Make your-self at home." Once, I spilled my tea on my computer but nothing happened to me or it at that time and so I did not stop.

A DREAM OF LALOO

What a girl or boy becomes by accident in the deep of the body, someone else's body, emerging to gasps: impossible service and far-off ends. Here I am speaking in fiscal terms of the hospital where the future of the girl is immediately obvious to the nurse, who reaches out with the needle to stop it, the hysterical reaction to the birth of a defective figure, but the mother says no, I want to see her. Put her on me. I want to hold her in the warm pool.

THE MANY COLORS OF LALOO

A cyborg is an iridescent pleat. No. I want to write opposites—saturations of opposite colors (silver and Coca-Cola) that make a person, like a fingerprint, obsessed with the liquor of patterning. This is more intense than painting in the best light in France or New Mexico. You could do it at night in your bedroom in Illinois. Un-illuminated. Like in India, when the electricity goes, two or three times a day, all monsoon. Your grandmother lights candles and pours the water over your bent head in the dark, glittery courtyard where you live, together.

I wrote about cyborgs on a balcony in fake Portugal (my kitchen, painted gold, orange, and red) in a pink dress unzipped at the back, ignoring the doorbell. After lunch, I commonly drank a tablespoon of whisky killed with mint leaves from the garden and sugar. Kill is the wrong word. An alcove, a sort of balcony. Analyzing cyborgs took imagination, loneliness, and liquid nourishment, which was the opposite of everyday life in a township with its outfits and specials: Baked Meatloaf Sandwich with Fries and Salad, $5.99. Three-quarter length jeans and a crisp white shirt and a multicolored cloth belt from Guatemala.

Here in the U.S., cyborgs reverse the basilar process, the occipital process, the process of change, which is pleating. A pleat is a fold. Unsticking her, my silver girl with her Pepsi eyelids, Laloo, I blessed her. I couldn't help it. Her skin was harsh and dry and so I took her to the doctor. There in the hospital, I let her check in individually, like a portion, while I went looking for something to eat, being a person from a town and thus reliant upon the almost daily intake of mountains of food. What follows is a beautiful story of the kind I'd relate to out-of-town guests on nights when the electricity failed and we had to eat dinner by candlelight and pee in the backyard. "Do you have health insurance? What is your social security number?" I'd been eating sauerkraut in the basement cafeteria and when I returned, she'd gone. "She left before we could sew her back up. She won't get far. Does she have health insurance, do you know? Do you know her social by any chance? Are you a blood relative? Do you need a clipboard? Here's a pen." I am writing this in a fluorescent kitchen, I mean foyer. There are magazines, elevators, and ladies with healthy-looking teeth. It must be something inside them that's the problem. Pans beneath each chair to collect the grease.

PLAN B

In a hospital write a suture. This is medical not special. Take notes about the body for two to six hours as if it were your employment, which it is, in the hospital. Soaping, SOAP chart: what you did, what you saw, what changed, what comes next for the structure at hand. Or operating: make slits, notice thickenings, and die. No. This is not a text to bring down the light. This is not the journey of a soul after death. This is the story of a bad girl who, concealing her interesting, blood-filled body beneath her coat, though it was summer, limped off, refusing medicine. What is a girl? It is an ancient office. Drops of blood on the asphalt of the parking lot. Dark-skinned, dressed for winter, a bulky parcel-like mass extending from her midsection, Laloo must avoid public transportation, which is scrutiny.

Something hurts. It's 7 p.m. when she heads for the highway. These are things I feel about cyborgs from a distance as if they are happening to me. I feel, for example, Laloo's scarlatina, the dark red color flooding her attachment sites. Something very natural is spreading through her body like a mechanism of rapid healing: the blood clotting on cue, the hair growing back thicker and darker than before but abnormally fast.

Hours not days. The day is monstrous for the cyborg as I imagine it—that feeling of being on the verge of a gastro-intestinal sickness but having to travel across three time zones before you are home. If not monstrous, then such a day is an experience of speed, as seen from above. From a plane: a car, glinting. The girl gets into the car. This is going, tracked from a separate source. Then it stops and I want that, what happens when the red girl gets out of the car, her teeth jammed together in a determined fashion. Laloo means red. Her arms are decorated with henna tattoos. Butterflies, etc. Paisley swirls. "Hey Red, where do you think you're going?" I like to think of her as ambient. Look. She's walking to the corner bodega to buy a green chile pork burrito. "Can I please have it with beans? Or whatever you think would taste good." Healed, she's ravenous. It's as if in spite of a major injury a patient has recovered her intellect, undisturbed by the extraction of a foreign body from the body. Her actual body. Locomotion and digestion, as functions, are intact. She could leave the hospital by nightfall if someone came to get her, because she's fragile, despite her miraculous re-formed state. No. The hospital is behind her like an edifice.

THIS IS A REAL BODY

Here, the body is generic. Red next to black. Raven-black, a dot turns the corner and disappears. Only under conditions of surveillance is the dot red like a pulsating bindi. It's her. It's Laloo moving outwards into fields. In a field there are cars and tall buildings, kind strangers and bad ones. The bad ones have cars.

"Do you mind if I ask you something? What's that red dot on your forehead?" Is it:

a) A gunshot injury.
b) A way to track your coming and goings.
c) Local custom.
d) Does it mean you're married? You're not married are you?
e) Fashionable or something.
f) Muslim. You're not Muslim are you?

Peeling the dot off her skin, Laloo sticks it on the mirror in the Conoco restroom. Here on the outskirts of Detroit, having escaped from the hospital and now the car. Not wanting to push it. "Maybe I'll have a frappuccino." These are her first words in the real world and they are happy ones, indicating that she has overcome the depression that usually follows medical contact plus a dodgy pick-up. Even John-boy had his jaunts, every Sunday morning in West Virginia/England. He got in his ratty blue truck and zoomed off at about 11 a.m., despite his mental collapse following a stint in the U.S. Army.

Surreptitiously, the woman taking Laloo's money affixes a red dot to her (Laloo's) coat sleeve as she hands her the change. "Would you like a bag for that?" "How far along are you?" Frowning, unresponsive, Laloo shoves the money in her back pocket and turns, her hand protectively cupping her protruding abdomen. On her way out, a wave of warm air comes into the shop. It is a tropical moment. On the monitor, even the customers can see her (Laloo) next to the road, under a streetlamp, shifting from foot to foot in a small cloud of insects. Occasionally, she takes a long pull of her coffee (flavored with three hazelnut, nondairy creamers), turning her head far to the left, as if advertising her unusually long throat, her ability to swallow, to the people in the passing cars.

TEXT TO

COMPLETE

A TEXT

Sex is always monstrous. Blood appears in the air next to the body but nobody asks a question about the body. "Please touch me there. More. Oh god." For a hitchhiker, the problem of the boudoir is transferred to a makeshift, itchy, unsafe space on the verge of a New Mexico highway. It is often the sex of another era, in which the socks and dress shirt/blouse are not necessarily removed.

I hitchhiked in the beginning because it seemed glamorous to me, ultra-American, like a Christian with an entrenched migraine who resorts to brand-name anti-inflammatories when prayer does not do the trick. At first, my encounters on the thoroughfares of your country were quotidian; after all, it is not really hitchhiking to buy a Greyhound ticket three weeks in advance then have a going-away party in a dorm with a banner and balloons. Again, this is an example of departure in another time. As a foreign student on a scholarship, it was an ordinary matter to file for an extension for the completion of a thesis on Salman Rushdie's early works. Nevertheless: "How can we keep tabs on these J1 visa holders, who come over here and . . . the university, as an institution, really needs to be more accountable. We need a database and we need a system of checks and balances to make sure any change of address is verified by at least two pieces of information. They need to do their course work and then they need to go home."

I didn't want to go home. This is a boring sentence. Perhaps for you Oregon is a calming word, evoking images of blackberry pie, ocean vistas, and the capture of suspected felons. I had never heard the word Oregon before. Like the distance of Scotland from London, it seemed impossibly far. A beautiful hazard: to go and keep going. How can I put this? In England, nobody ever, ever, ever did this. I, who once drove straight to Glasgow with a thermos of instant coffee mixed with milk and sugar, in a dinged-up Datsun Cherry, was considered an anomaly. "Are you demented? Why do you want to drive in a car to bloody Scotland? It's seven hours on the M1, man!" Though, outwardly, I was wan and somewhat reticent, I . . . no, I was. My sexual experience consisted of lying under an elm tree in Hyde Park at the age of seventeen and being told by an undergraduate student of the London School of Economics that my breasts in that position, from that angle, resembled two fried eggs. We were meeting in a park as per the era. I am sure contemporary Punjabi-British teenagers are fearless individuals, undaunted by the prospect of community censure. Back then we met by the iron-wrought gate on a park bench, on a path built for seventeenth-century promenades. It is always a century. In my century, sex was a field of restraint and intensity unsurpassed by anything except drinking coffee in a foreign country like Scotland or Wales and borrowing my father's car forever. "Are you out of your bleeding head? Your dad's going to skin you alive!" .

In some senses, this (driving) is the opposite of hitchhiking, in which the interior of the car is always unfamiliar. The day was real in a different way back then, in the way that it sensitized me to risk, a kind of twin to permission. Two black swans: that day and this one, history and fiction, what I went for and what I really wanted, which I didn't know until I got there by which time it was impossible to consider the long journey home as either practical or sensible, considering the trouble I was already in and the rain, which had started to come down in a series of reddish sheets; the streetlamps were pink.

On Prince Street, in Glasgow, I saw the sign for American style pizza and went down the steps to the basement café. The tables were coated with green plastic. There was hot tea, which the waitress slung down my gullet with a funnel as I focused my eye on a laminated print of a white, blocky rose with a pink dot at its center. "Charles Rennie Mackintosh," said the waitress, pronouncing "osh" so that it rhymed with horse. "Are you from India?" "Would you like some jam with that scone? I bet they don't have scones in India, do they?" "More tea? I heard you have a lot of tea, over there, isn't that right?"

Plan b: The extension of my throat. The euphoria of theft. Other countries with their sayings and beliefs. The original plan, formulated by my father during his morning commute across London: marrying a British-born Hindu Brahmin dentist with brown skin, but not too brown, and rosy cheeks. Note on the mantelpiece, tucked behind the marble figurine of Shiva: what is forthcoming under the original plan? Extraction? What kind of sex is possible on the dentist's chair late at night for that girl, your girl, who nervously asks for a blanket? She has her socks on. She's shivering. It is sometimes sex when you touch yourself beneath the proffered blanket clearly not washed between patients, but in this scene the limbs of the dentist's young Asian bride are rigid and smell faintly of wintergreen-scented nail polish or mouthwash. Dad, "please don't swallow." Rinse then spit. Spit then swallow.

I could not go home and so, after a brief visit to the Hill House —Charles Rennie Mackintosh's art deco home on the Firth of Clyde, where he painted geometric rosebuds forever in a kind of frenzy, as it seemed from the décor—I turned left and kept driving. I drove my car into the Atlantic and kept driving, my chest very tight beneath the surface. It was difficult to feel anything or really to see, and so I can only say that I went into a damaging ocean. This is going. Damaged, washed up on the mythical shores of New Jersey a few days later, my car failed to start. This is later, when the car stopped, and, looking up from my hands, white-knuckled on the steering wheel, I realized that I was okay.

Now I am here, in the future of color. I'm sorry I do not have more to say about the period of submergence that preceded my arrival. I am not interested in it. I do not recall it. I . . . It was only when my car stopped that I realized what I had to do, on my own terms, with my own two legs: get going. Is that how you say it? Get up and go. The destiny of my body as separate from my childhood: I came here to hitchhike. I came here to complete a thing I began in another place. Removing wet pages from my rucksack, I lay them on the shore, securing them with beautiful shells and pebbles. When they dried, I folded them into squares and put them in my pocket, next to my body. Misshapen, exhilarated, I said get. I said go. Get up now and go. "Are you okay?" "Do you need a ride somewhere?" "Let me look in the trunk. I might have something in there. Here you go. You're shivering! Do you need to go to the hospital? At least let me buy you a cup of coffee."

SOME AUTOBIOGRAPHICAL INFORMATION ABOUT CYBORGS

Laloo means red because Lal means red, so Laloo means "the red one." It is a masculine, sun-like name of Vedic origin but I cannot change that. My alien number is A#786334901. My social security number is 102-70-5846. My phone number is 970-290-6292. Please call me and tell me what the difference is between a monster and a cyborg. I need to know. Also, you can e-mail me at beatricehastogo@yahoo.com. It is a bit better for me if you e-mail as I am at heart a hitchhiker and sometimes out of range for cell reception. For breakfast I eat whatever comes to hand. Berries. Nuts. Roadside vegetables such as asparagus and . . . I can't think of any other vegetables. This is the story of how I became a red girl, which sounds bad, but I don't know how else to say it. I turned red over the course of my journeys. To put it another way, I changed from one kind of girl to another as a result of my experiences. Is that a boring thing to say? I think all girls can say that and so I am not sure if my story is a particularly useful one to refer to as an example of physical transformation generated by new environments. Perhaps it is simplest if I begin with images of pregnancy and birth, complete with details of perverse, pregnant-lady appetites—"Honey, I need pickles and a strawberry milkshake, pronto!"—or the mechanics of a prolonged gestation moved along by sexual acts of all kinds, but nobody wants that, not even me. It is nauseating, for example, to think of that syringe of bull semen; indeed, I am not sure if mating is something that happens before someone is born or after, in the space of the future, and so I will leave that to you, the larger sense of a bodily organization: its complex workings and ways of communicating across systems. That is research and it is beautiful, but sometimes I think the red is fading and so I want to write these things down while the blood is in the line. The line is a sentence but also a hand. My friend, a medical intuitive from Iowa City, reads palms and hypnotizes you to find out what is happening inside your body. Specifically, she analyzes the horizontal lines that transect the mount of mercury, the plump bit of flesh at the base of the little finger, for the one that is the reddest. If a particular line is red, it means you love someone. The red is obviously from blood which is directed by internal, occult means to a place in your hand. Your hand, in turn, throbs with blood as you ask the question, "Does she/he love me?" My friend takes your hand in hers and tracks that blood with a sharp eye; when she closes her eyes and describes what she sees, it is as if an unseen hand has reached down into the world of matter and touched something there, where it is not meant to be touched. A body is meant to be mysterious but I can't tell if the vividness of the blood amplifies this mystery or reduces it. "What's going to happen? Will I be loved without reserve to the end of my days? When will I die?" She touches me and sees things. Then it is narration or storytelling and I am okay, until it's time to go and I'm left alone with the terrible, associative, almost monstrous images, of a birthing woman in distress. "Abortion by mouth." "Ultimate fate of viable ectopic children." These are nineteenth-century images of obstetric anomalies; I see these divergent things in what she says about the blurry places of my chest and abdomen. Fine.

IMAGES OF PREGNANCY AND BIRTH IN LALOO'S WORDS

I. WHEN I WAS BORN

When I was born, they did not know whether to wrap me in a pink blanket or a green one. Was I born cyborg or something else, something more towards a human being with its job opportunities and ways of loving across gender? I don't know. It's hard even for a trained technician to interpret the number and extent of my brain's convolutions or sulci—the complex folds that are markers for different intensities of intellect. Even a limited analysis would resolve the issue of mechanical identity. When does a chimp become a man? Is a Punjabi more related to the citizens of Greece, racially, than to those of Kerala or Tamil Nadu, who have different shaped noses? I've been diagnosed as either girl—black or pink, etc.—depending on the nurse I mean doctor/how much the doctor has drunk I mean smoked. I come from an era—the

1970s—in which even the orderlies smoked Winstons in the elevator. As a child visiting the hospital for my yearly check-up, I sat in my wheelchair, which I didn't need—I was just having my blood drawn—but they said it was free (the wheelchair), a service offered by the hospital authorities to anyone who expressed a need. So I took it. I took the opportunity to rest my limbs. I was born with more than one arm, more than one leg. How about them apples? No, I'm confused. This was England. Everything is free in England, if you are a child and Margaret Thatcher is still a butcher's daughter on the verge of womanhood; even the milk and biscuits are free.

Bloody hell. I can't delay this any longer. Do you have a pen? Can I have some foam with that, and sprinkles? Okay, I'm ready. Let's go. See how American I've become? Coffee. A generalized, low-grade feeling of discontent like a farm animal who knows in its little pig/sheep/turkey/lamb/baby-cow heart that it's running out of options as the cold weather approaches. I even think twice before going in for a complimentary wellness assessment. I think about the money. I think about what they did last time I was there, in the outpatient clinic, for a routine examination: images of which are re-triggered simply by leaning over the water fountain in a waiting room. These places and experiences are sites of infection even in this day and age. It's disgusting. The nurses routinely leave the pig valves in a bucket in plain view outside the restroom, without any consideration of what that might mean, to a client. A patient is a client. How about *them* apples? Red apples with red cheeks. All they need is a shoelace for a tail, two raisins for the eyes: bake at 350 degrees, ignoring the smell of burning plastic. (The ends of the shoelaces in this country are protected, I've noticed, by little transparent hoods. If I were a child, I could suck them off, nibble them off with my little teeth.)

To summarize: What is the relationship of memory to what pleases? This is the story of how I changed my structure. "All structure is relationship." Those are not my words. This is not my beautiful gingerbread house. Ida Rolf, *Rolfing and Physical Reality.* How a monster remembers things when she's worked on. Rolfed. Integrated. Trauma therapies of all kinds, especially the ones related to flickering, re-patterned eye movements. It was a home birth. Everyone knows that cyborgs are born in hospitals.

2. RELATIONSHIP OF MEMORY TO WHAT PLEASES: IMAGES OF MY CHILDHOOD MIXED WITH THE ACTUAL BIRTH

1. Somatic forms of memory: Once again, the year dissolves into numbers. The rooms are already half full with water.

We live at the opening of the Narrows. The morning is, at six, already silver. I am given pleasure by, am put into boats by: the first really overcast morning of the western summer. The spongy heat reminds me of Punjabi mornings, early monsoon, when our mothers are awake by four to soak the gacky curd in a muslin rag over the sink, for raw cheese, before it turns. I wake to dripping, deep in my ears.

But this slow, too-dark softness of the light-coming-into-things reminds me of London mornings, when you wake up and go straight out to get *The Guardian* from Balfours for your dad. Taking the back way home through the park, which is heavy with the chocolate and silver stripes of the wet bark of plum trees. The plums are very hard still, with a fine, white dust on them despite the previous night's rain. I don't know. My teeth flinch after the first bite.

11. Memory stemming from Hakomi-based analysis in warm rooms on the fifth floor of a building with cacti in the lobby:

Your father stalking around the house in a white vest and drawstring boxers, looking for a pen to do the crossword. "Why can't I ever find a bloody pen around here?" My father wrote columns. My mother sewed shifts. I had dozens of sisters who came from these shifts and columns, to produce entities somewhere between the two. Some of us were abandoned at birth: too pointy, or the belly too sunken in, or the eyes themselves without stems. Born with yellow eyes whose roots extended to my liver, I was permitted to live. Though, within a few hours of my first breath, I had to sign a form guaranteeing that I would behave like a normal human child. They held my tiny, pink fingers around the pencil and moved my hand in the motion of a primitive cross: x for baby. Years later, when I could speak and write, I chose this sentence as my first: "Can you hear me? Am I making sense?" Though they came upon my words in the diary I kept beneath my pillow, they were considered a waste. Worse: immoral. Thus, they hung me by my legs from a louvered window. Segregated, if I think of the window as four wet shelves slanting down; like that. They cut her, the four. A case without parallel. A girl displaying vigor as she flails. This was surely monstrous to onlookers, to people passing by on the streets below and looking up in horror.

III. Memory wherein there's no relation between experienced events recalled during rolfing:

"Let me know if it hurts." My womb, bed sheets, a man's dark, age 21, I mean page 21: write the first four sentences. This is a bibliographical enterprise. Fabulous index: all you have to do is open the book at random. Close your eyes, and your finger lands on "Postal routes" or "Yesterday had a man in it" or "scattering the ashes" or "reduced to spotless." Could you go a bit deeper? I can take a lot of pressure. Oh yeah. Right there. "This is the most reasonable solution." Rolfing: I'm buttery. The rolfer slips a finger into my body in a professional capacity. Are my ligaments rubbery? You betcha. "Fifty dollars please." Driving away, I find myself chewing the edge of my appointment card. "Tuesday the 4th. 5 p.m." Define Tuesday. Inherit Tuesday. On Tuesdays, in London, our Hanuman shrine in the kitchen window was daubed with vermillion powder. That is red, like me. My mother fasted until 6 p.m., when my dad came home from work. My sisters offered the bowl, pestle, and spoon to Hanuman in a brief gesture of please or yes, then set to work threshing the corn into fine flour for the evening chapatis. My father was very bad-tempered and so my sisters worked through occasional bouts of intense abdominal pain without a murmur. A trickle. Privately, they complained of violent spasms like those experienced in labor. Discharge of bones with what was coming out already. The bones were tiny. Once I saw a human hand, no bigger than a grape, crumpled up yet obviously that. In a wet place. On the floor. I was little but I set to work with a bucket and some sudsy water. Now my back hurts. "Would you like to buy a package? I can offer you a discount of up to 20%."

3. MY SPECIFIC FEARS:
IMAGES PRECEDING CHILDBIRTH

Waking I remember my dreams, as one who is fearful remembers being nine, the age a girl is, in Ludhiana or Southall, when she is scared for the first time, of shiny things. Even the kettle is composed of surfaces: glass and going; little human eyes bouncing off the maple veneer of the kitchen units then through the door and down the hall. There in a back room is an impossible scene: a kind of birthing action. "A child already dead is dying." Fine.

But also, horribly: that my papers are not in order. That my bottle of sweet almond oil has spilled, making the official stamp indecipherable. Where am I? Hitchhiking, deep in a different day. It is a different day but I can't stop the quality. The insides of my arms have zigzags. Out the little finger. Nevertheless, I clutch my British passport, waving its gold-embossed and maroon packaging at the oncoming traffic, hoping a car will slow down and open. Please help me. I say these things wordlessly, with my body, a kind of rendering on the side of the road.

Highway 66. It's night but also day. 5 a.m. This is the next country with its humid climate and green light. I wake up early in an irrigation canal, fall leaves in my hair, to this other light in which even the faces of loved ones, awake or not awake, are imminent. It is dream-like to travel like this. Orwellian. George Orwell taught grammar-school English at the Mellow Lane Primary School in Hayes, Middlesex, where I competed in a county-wide Scottish-dancing competition in 1978.

Och. I am not wanting to forget what it was like, to live in a fifties council block sprawl on the outskirts of thrombosis/ The Royal Opera posters on the tube/people who ate marmalade

47

and roast beef for dinner ... a pencil always behind my ear or in my hair, for protection. Pen. Paintbrush.

> When I walk amongst thy
> When I tryst with
> Eat with

These are not my kind. Before I came to your country, I donated my Arden Shakespeares to the Romanian Orphans Second-hand Shop in Ruislip Manor. Gutted yet certain of the basic nobility and correctness of my charitable actions, I went to the Portuguese café under the station. There, I ordered a macchiato and drank it facing the wall pretending it was Portugal. Where I was. A balcony. And wrote: "Ach. In marrying, I will make a cyborg offspring." That is separate. There in a fake country, I made a list of specific fears:

1. I fear for my children's children. 2. Not even when eating my breakfast of black coffee and fried okra am I steadfast. 3. Listen, I tell my bridegroom, "This is a different day. I want to have it in a hospital! I do not want to have a natural birth."

4. MEMORY IS A WALL: IMAGES OF MOTHERHOOD IN A MEDICAL SETTING, WITH BLACK COFFEE COMING FROM THE OVERHEAD FAUCET IN THE CAFÉ LIKE FAKE BLOOD IN A BLACK-AND-WHITE FILM. I CAN SAY WHATEVER I WANT.

Childhood memory: my mother had red hair, in the photos I painted over, with vermillion acrylic. My mother, an Indian. My mother, in the dust and heat; *heat is good,* she says, *it washes you.* So I am walking to the highway to catch the express bus to Connaught Circle. (I walked to the bus stop every Saturday morning, to catch the number ninety-eight to Harlington, Middlesex, for my piano lesson.) I was seven years old. (I was bleeding heavily.) It was so hot. May, late May, maybe June, in the northern hemisphere. The dark nurse stuck a needle in my hip. (These child-bearing hips.) My mother said: *you'll be late.* And she handed me my Berlioz. (My sarong.) I was seventeen. And I wound it tight. And the sun went into my body and made it wrong.

(Chopin. Grieg.) Mad dogs, the lot of them. (They take my British passport to verify my living body.) They stick things in. Faster.

Memory of the earth: Paris; not Paris itself, but the cup of treacly espresso, set down upon the albino linen, in the nighttime. A man or a woman, it doesn't matter. All I remember are the brutal, bright hands of the barista, pushing my cup across the counter. (Zinc of the body, when it lies face down, on the zinc: the hand I mean. A palm. So many lines, splitting off as they approach the thenar eminence, mount of venus, thickened pad of grids. *In your mid-twenties, you'll leave and never come back.* So many crossings, in the invisible layers that are multiple as a boa's. I mean a cobra's.

Kraits. Palimpsest: not Paris itself, but a few days when I had a specific, temporary skin. A sea-bell tolling in the open window of the café.) Someone—my wife? My husband?—said: "I have gold on my finger and wool on my feet." (The atoms of gold. The atoms of feet. A storm is coming from the north.) Returning to me as water:

The oxygen of other times;

having loosened, off the surface, from a little touch. In passing; the stranger. (I will drink him. He will drink me. He drinks her. She drinks him. I am drinking: the hands that give me coffee, for nothing, on a Thursday evening in the Latin Quarter, when it's raining and I am so obviously a tourist.)

5. A LACK OF HUMAN RESOURCES: IMAGES OF WALKING AIMLESSLY THROUGH A CITY, PLUS CONCEPTION.

I don't even have an origin myth. Just places where I stood, at crosswalks, waiting for people to start moving/disappearing; angling my vision so that I did not have to look directly at my subject, the person crossing in the opposite direction. (Not wanting to terrify.)

Neither is my grasp of stasis: adequate. No words that suit for "the anthropology of spirals." It is, all in all, a bunch of mangy shite that I have stopped in. And I don't even have a hanky.

All I have is a series of lovers who want *all* the normal things. "Bite my hand off." "Hold open my eyelids until I puke." "Tenderly." When they fall asleep, they always ask for a story. The only stories I remember are my mother's, but in my own Queen's English to make them plausible to the American ear:

In the beginning, there was a big light. No, it wasn't an American Spirit. It was Durga, the goddess of the second millennium. As a consequence of her explosive arrival, she gave birth to three sons: Shiva, Brahma, and Vishnu. In order to create a future or further progeny, she knew she would have to have sex with her own children, as there was no one else about right then. When she asked Vishnu and Brahma if they wanted to mate with her, they refused. So she slit their throats. Shiva, not being a stupid boy, agreed to a perfunctory lovemaking, but only on the condition that she restored his brothers to life. Durga called her sons up out of the dead, then turned around three times in an oval of light, emerging as three brides—Lakshmi, Sarasvati, and Parvati. In this way, light, in-

verting itself, was able to triple, then turn into six, which led to many ecstatic couplings for quite some time. This all came to an end when a blustery old man with a long white beard hurtled down from the mountain, claiming to be Parvati's father. Nobody knew what to say, so he grabbed her and chopped her into many pieces before their eyes, shouting something about the shame she had brought onto him and his family and how he was going to fry her up in a skillet. It was a bit odd, because all his relatives looked just like him: pale-faced grizzlers with a brilliant grasp of the early works of Matthew Arnold. When Shiva, Parvati's husband, found out, he was very angry. Galloping to the crime scene on a zebra with its skin peeling off in long tatters revealing the musculature beneath, he went from place to place weeping, scooping up and gathering the pieces of his wife's body. For some time, he rubbed her limbs and organs over his own body, bloodying himself and singing songs that nobody knew how to translate. And then very early one morning, he threw the dismembered parts to the ten directions, and wherever they fell, a mountain grew. And now people go to these mountains for picnics. There's been quite a problem with deforestation.

"Oh Momma, another one pleasepleaseplease!"

Or: "You be the mummy and I'll be the little boy. I'm a naughty little boy."

Or: "Honestly, darling, your vocabulary has really gone down the bog since you've been in America. *Picnics? Grizzlers?* I think you need to come home immediately."

6. NOSTALGIA: IMAGES FROM THE
EARLY CHILDHOOD OF A CYBORG (ME).

Monkey Island, Maidenhead, England, 1977

"But Mummy, where are the monkeys?"

"Somewhere. Maybe under those bushes. Why don't you go and look for them?"

[Looking for monkeys that did not exist.]

Jaipur, India, 1981

"Mummy, do monkeys eat chapatis?"

"Of course they do. You're a monkey. I'm a monkey. We all came from monkeys, and we eat chapatis, don't we?"

"Yes, but I'm scared."

"Go on, darling. They won't bite you."

[Getting bitten by vicious monkeys who had yellow teeth, and having to have shots.]

Regents Park Zoo, London, England, 1982

"Madam, would you please desist from doing that. Excuse me? Madam? Please stop your child from doing that. Madam, I think it would be best if you moved on to the next enclosure."

[Being kicked out of the primate enclosure, after being found with my mother, by the zoo-keeper, making faces at the chimps and generally inciting them to fling themselves against the hypothetically unbreakable glass wall between us.]

7. HOW I REMEMBER THINGS: INTER-LUMINAL IMAGE

A purple latex glove on the asphalt.

8. FURNISHINGS: IMAGES OF LOSS,
OF KNOWING YOURSELF TO BE A BABY

A bottle of milk pulled with a string and spilled in London. There on the tar.

Protests. Race riots: Wogs versus Skinheads. These atmospheres were textural to the time I lived in. As a cyborg baby, suspended by my ankles from a louvered window by my father, I saw these images in reverse: a kind of streaming spotted with whiteness.

9. I GO AWAY: ANCESTRAL IMAGES OF BLEEDING

Red dust, by July, makes a thick paste up past my ankles. This is a different country. Elderly men weep when they see me, commenting later upon my resemblance to their dead cousin, Shanta, who bled to death on a pilgrimage to a Kali temple in the foothills above Nangal. When my mother tells me this later, I immediately know that she (my doppelganger) died of shame. "She had her menses and still she went, even though she was bleeding. Suddenly, she complained of a stomachache and by the time her Mummy and Daddy came from the village, she was dead." This is an ancestral image of blood but also a face. Cramping, I reach for the coffee, exacerbating my symptoms.

10. THE LAST TRIMESTER: IMAGES OF WATER IN A HUMAN BODY

I've passed from point to point, my pleasures coming in increments, like electrons. Basis. It's August. My waters are fit to burst: sticking a finger in myself the easy option. Living this hitchhiking life in the land of known mutilators, I'm conscious that one day soon I'll accept a ride from someone who wants to eat me up, rinsing his mouth with Coke then spitting, to remove the taste of my body.

Possible occupations not requiring proof of health insurance or a permanent address:
1. Translator of the INS home page for Punjabi and Somali cab drivers in New York City.
2. Can't think of anything else.

Bloated, yet compressed: I'm in the thing just before the other thing. Perhaps one day I will live in a community with others. Application is being processed. Yep. Soon, I will hold the laminated object in my paw, to proffer to potential employers. "Temporary-permanent." This is status but how will it reach me? Is there a poste restante in Eugene, Oregon? It is difficult to eat well when you are hitchhiking. All that salt and sugar can't be good for the pancreas, let alone the heart.

II. POST-PARTUM REALITY: HOW THE MILK GOES BAD

Ideas for daytime activities during a time of great stress:

1. To say how it ends. The day. Unimaginable daily rituals. Brie on a stoneware plate. Underwear made of combed cotton. A cat called Silky Malone.

2. The day itself. Five cups of over-sweet espresso. No lemon rind on the side. It's getting harder and harder to stand up. This isn't Europe. I think I am going to die on the sidewalk outside a hospital.

3. Sometimes I think I am traveling to the sea in order to rebound inland. Or that I have a stone's destiny, with a stone's outcome of sinking, midair, into the amazing water between us. The midwest is one big, shallow lake bed—a depression visible in satellite photographs—that occasionally floods. Thus: Chicago. A room belonging to someone's daughter, who is away studying in Boston, at Tufts, until June. I imagine a rather vibrant teenage

squirrel, with pink toenail polish, and an extensive, untested German vocabulary. Each night, I shove her quota of fuzzy bunnies and spooky dolls off the quilted counterpane with its cheeky pattern of cherries and bananas. My hosts bring me warm milk. It's a little odd, that they both have to bring it, but I live rent-free. A reprieve from constant travels. They don't know it but I'm pregnant. I am going to masturbate all night to make it happen: the terrible spasms that predicate nocturnes. By nocturne I mean baby. Chopin for babies. I turn up the radio to drown out the noises I have to make, to make it real: contraction, expulsion, fate.

4. As a baby, I rejected my mother's fluid—it was blue!—so they (my parenting figures) had to get their Welsh landlady, Catherine Eccleston, my hero in her pink cashmere and dark green, dog-haired kilt, to spoon-feed me Nestle's condensed milk straight from the tin.

12. CLONE-CLONE RELATIONS: IMAGES OF MATING

We fuck each other blind on the pre-ordained shag, the backs of living ewes, what do we know? Dolly's first shearing: our soft bed. Two identical beings, twinning on the relative ground, for the viewing pleasure of our "friends and family." Home video #2068, entitled: "Stabilizes." Whatever that means.

Have you ever kissed yourself in the mirror, leaving oil/butter smears? Have you ever put your finger inside your own body?

Two fingers, in two places? Three fingers, in three places? Like that, except, in our case, when we fall asleep, they take swabs from our thighs. When we grow up, they tell us we were "silvered" by our own fathers, and that this is why we can't do it, choose metal, with other men. Water not metal. Distorted ice crystals with the words "Suck it and die" pasted to our drinking vesicles. Our trumpets. Our shoes. Our chipped teacup from Sheffield, and the plastic funnel from Glasgow. My memory, we say to our gynecologists, is not what it was. There are sexual bruises, for example, that we can't explain to the nurse. She gives us some folic acid, a year's supply of Pampers, and a pack of Marlboro Lights.

13. BEYOND THE BODY: WHAT IF I GET PREGNANT?

"A year or so later, we give birth to children twinned at the palms." This is an example of a cyborg giving birth to a monster, which is really bad. The strange baby is the opposite direction to a human baby, the kind with almost symmetrical features; no, that's unclear, I mean it is furry. Fur is skin: the resilient pouch a human sleeps in, morning, noon, and night. A cyborg progresses the biology; a monster refuses its future, just as chimps go mad in zoos and can't be trusted with children, even when they've been rehabilitated in the special retirement camp in Florida. "Then, in our post-partum dementia, we go shoplifting." In the attempt to leave Sears Roebuck with a yellow umbrella, a brown nylon skirt with elasticated waistband, and some Long Island bridesmaid-esque costume seed pearls, we are stopped at the door by a man in a black suit and Ray Bans. There's a big fight. We tear the man to pieces, but then our babies are taken away by an orderly. Actually, unbeknownst to the hospital, he takes them home to his grandmother, who cares for them in turns. The orderly is in heaven and waits for them to grow up. Marry him. Kiss him. Whatever. He is a sick bastard. Look at his white sneakers.

For the rest of our lives, we try to come up with reasonable explanations for our behavior, should our children ever seek us out. This is in England, in Heathrow Airport's Terminal Four. Our employer. Yet a portal. We keep our eye upon the arriving tourists. They are exhausted. They are vulnerable. Sometimes a child wanders into our area, which we are under strict instructions to clean at twenty-minute intervals.

Is it you? Come to mama.

14. MAKE IT NEW (DON'T TELL):
IMAGES, PRE-CONCEPTION

The face above me is blurry. It says I have to hold my neck like this and when I don't ... don't do it ... exactly right, there is a terrible silence. I came out of that silence towards you like a black swan. Have you seen that warm pond in England? The Thames nourishes it and in the summer it is choked with lilies. Flies and swans.

Instead of bread we took stale chapatis, as a family, to throw to the birds that were migrating from Russia to Spain, or were clipped. Ornamental. I was walking with my family and our family friends. I recognize that face. I eat that swan.

15. IN THEIR RELATION TO SKIN: MORE IMAGES FROM THE MATING SCENE

Claustrophobia: accepting coffee. Saying yes to tea. When I go into the café, it's already no good. The doorway. A nervousness my skin can't accommodate. Sweat: proof. *Lick me.*

In New York City, I say yes to the man who is red with brown stripes, the one who cuts my hair into papery thin slices. On the corner. In an old place with sawdust on the floor. I mean ham. With black and white tile, which is shiny. Every day I purchase makings.

This day, a Tuesday, Hanuman's day, he asks me if I will. (Sugar. Cream. What difficulties can coffee bring, brings. Besides the leaching of calcium many years hence, when I am already dead: The love of a butcher.) His knee, his bald head; a minimalism. That is his blue torn knee. His hair is so black. Hellohello, he says, like a British policeman. And already my skin starts ticking, getting wetter and wetter, which is bad. PLEASE MAY I HAVE SOME

PORK. PLEASE COULD YOU CUT OFF THE FAT. He asks me if I'd like to go for a walk by the river, to see the river. Doesn't he know those are two different things? Doesn't he understand that my skin is just a lining without anything beneath it? He does. Look at his eyes. He does indeed, and so I relax, profoundly, avoiding eye contact in a sort of dreamy old dream.

Come closer, he says. *Take off your clothes.* I say: your hands are too real. He says: *what?* I say: I can't have sex like a vegetable. He says: *what are you going on about now?* I think: but what will happen when he cuts me? What will happen to my black discs? My red jelly? What will he think when he sees my knickers? They got holes in them. They're not frilly.

16. THE BIRTH: IMAGES OF THE BIRTH AND OF MY MOTHER'S LIFE BEFORE SHE MET MY FATHER

Coming slowly. The usual metals—cadmium yellow, enamel chipping, salty timberline nails for keeping trees in place (where they could blacken or curl, i.e., the upper slope)—cleave. Imagine a mine, its pools opal with copper. Making the paper wet like that is work.

This being occurs at the center of fear. Where a woman is very frightened at a pining table in the far kitchen late at night: in three minutes, she will call a ranger. If the man comes home and she is not a black woman (the color of *this* is white, where she comes from; she'll marry in red): then there *is* no birth. Nobody comes out of the crossing. A long wait. I sip my Bud, skim the second diary of Virginia Woolf. *Writing must be formal.* November 18, 1924. Don't I know that already, somehow, waking early with the dogs, stuffing paper in my pocket, a pen in my hair. This morning, I found a nest. When I bent to smell it, it smelled of seaweed; fleshiness in a tide pool, mashed cup of the blue internal—ink, jelly, salt. *Then.*

At the first juncture. First entry into space that turns in upon. When one's body disassembles itself into its known parts, returning wholly only after the fire sacrifice, the binding ceremony—

A grinding of, the cognition of . . .

When all the words for the divinity of the spongy crust fail, one after another. The cyborg says: "oggie." The invented word for horse. "Crane." Crane. "Hector Theater." Theatre. (The backlit ochre of the "mother" already fading.) There will be complete darkness by nightfall. As in the first stories her "father" told her at bedtime, of the volcano goddess, and the young man with the dripping Spanish knife standing at the rim.

The birth itself: an absence of genius, because the mind is in all things. (The genius flanks of Cherokee the horse, fabulous machines heaving steel to the top story, glittery *The Balcony* by Jean Genet, who had eyes all over his skin.)

At least, that's what happened/what they told me. But I have proofs: recorded loops, transparent sheets, permanent markers, the genetic memory of wooded places that men did not return from, green sidewalk chalk, and a black room without windows.

Entering through a slit, you can see tree after tree, projected and scratched onto six surfaces. After six minutes, enough to make you a little panicky, you will hear a brush-wind wooing. After six minutes, you will hear words. The trees, speaking.

Doesn't have to be trees.

17. THE HOUSE OF WATERS:
IMAGES OF THE WATER BREAKING

I came here, looking for food. A metal I could push into my opening: the first stoma, pink around the edges, able to rotate slightly.

(Speaking of the future: a blue tongue, from sucking on gumballs. A yellow palm, from licking sherbert—6 ounces for 6p, in a white paper bag no bigger than my hand—)

I went in, asking to see the jars they kept on a high shelf. Remembering myself a girl, stained with elements.

THE COLORS OF THE WORLD ARE ITS ELEMENTS.

(They said.) (A girl's hand.)
(A real girl.)

Instead, when they opened the door and sucked me in, it was a room I'd been in before: a waiting room (the faint smell of vinegar and baking soda, and a chewed-up chart of the body, tacked to a peeling wall. *A green line goes under, resurfacing in the eye.* What passes for the eye. No speckled jelly as such). A room with no obvious exits. Even the walls were loosening their valences, beginning to waver, turning to gold. Off-gold. "Reduced to spotless." *Mud* walls whose surfaces belonged to the plantar surfaces of human hands. I could see finger marks, whorls. Once, I was a living being, embellished with skin: fortunate and blighted in turns. I turned. In circles. In the adventure playground, which was concrete. When I fell, the nurse daubed me with yellow smears, that stung.

IODINE, ASPHALT, the crisp white underbelly of the woman above me. Already, I knew it. Could see it coming: (her apron fused to her thighs). The differential between the outer-metal, or linen, husks, and the converse organs, the under-tender: diminishing. Gone. I am here now. A bit hungry. When I go in to eat. When I am offered by strangers. I am a little bit, I am rather ... It goes like this: I open the door. I knock on the door. Someone comes, or does not come. I go in. To some extent, I am a woman. *Who are you?* they say, when I give them what I have. And *then* it breaks. Comes out of their mouths like brine. And in one version of what happened to me in the house of waters, I'm able to breathe in the absence of oxygen.

18. THE BIRTH GOES WRONG: DISTRESSING IMAGES

"Where I live, there are no human beings. Just eyes, arranged on shelves, according to color. The eyes that are blue, with some red-brown in them, are kept in an aluminum bucket by the door, for future sorting." —A girl

Something has happened. Such a silence. I DO NOT KNOW HOW TO LEAVE THIS PLACE. Cut through. I want to cut myself out of the future. "Oh shut up. Push harder," says the nurse with the needle dripping semen on my thigh on behalf of the hospital. The first girl I pushed out had brown eyes. I did not have names for her. I thought of her as my digestive system. Something once inside no longer in. Pushing and waving like tentacles. She had her own agenda though, and took off for Vegas with its exotic, inexpensive sushi buffets. She was an advanced infant.

And at the center: shimmering gelatin. Too beautiful to eat. Gagging, I saw some edge, in the form of a rope, between two citizens. I mean girls. Though I am a British citizen, they are not. They are from this place. Good. I have come to this country without practical forms of sustenance. My crappy suitcase from Ludhiana—blue, rigid, with pop-up locks and a little gold key, smeared with multiple originating tags—is stuffed with scraps: a Royal Doulton teapot, wrapped in pages of *The Sun*. Eight spiral notebooks with their oral histories of passage from Lahore to Nangal. A photograph of my father and my mother, though their faces and clothes are almost completely dissolved from the oils of fingers. Just an eye left, and a shoe. One blue and one brown. Clean underwear, etc. A shell I found by the sea, in the pristine, sentimental, freezing moments before I left my life behind me, forever. It was raining and I was naked.

Leaving, going, and being: they rock me and bind me with white cotton strips like a mummy. My nurses. My many mothers, in a series of almost imperceptible flickers. Lids. The glottal balls of the aqueous vitreous. This is a memory of my body as a cyborg girl or adult woman. A body; bake it. Eat it with cream. No. This is America. Make it two scoops of vanilla. No. Will I love and be loved in return? White people are so tricky. I want that special love. I want that eager mouth, all wet and spooky with ice cream. I want that day in which, unbound, sticky, and bruised, as if from plastic surgery, I am half a woman and half something else. A red girl with four arms: waving my arms in the photograph of my birth and thus recorded, accidentally, as an avatar of childhood and not a child herself with her organs inside her body like the other children.

19. SOFT CRAZINESS: VISUAL MEMORIES, POST-OP

I was a monster but the surgeon said no. You have your mother's eyes. My mother, smiling euphorically, smoothed the aluminum foil over the pillow and went to sleep, dreaming of mechanical sheep flying through a sky of tungsten. Copper and tulle. This thing she pushed off. This "but in the air." This "but the air changes your body." It was me. We communicated in silence. Then I left: a descent. Soft craziness. Drifts of freeable matter. I was three months old but I did it, I rolled out of bed. I rolled out the door and I rolled through London in the deep of the night until I reached the river. There, in the Thames, was a black swan with an orange nub on his beak. I think he had wings. I rolled into the water and bobbed there a few moments, like an olive or a rose or a dog, until he saw me and came over to where I was with great force. By my neck he took me in his beak and put me on his back. Then the ocean. How small we are, in this image, my mother, Mr. Swan, and I. There is an incredible sense of openness: a luminous intensity in which darkness has a part. When it rained, hours into our long journey to America, I saw citron-yellow flashes in the sky. I reached my little hand out as if taking the light in, through my palm, then touched the long neck of the black swan, feeling his muscles contract then relax as he moved farther out into the environment. "Hungry. Want naan. Want chole. Want dudhoo. (Yeast-free bread, chickpea curry, and milk.) Are we there yet?" I have a cousin in Elizabeth, New Jersey. As children in India, we washed our feet each morning beneath a pump. At night, when the electricity went out, our grandmother poured oil into little earthenware cups then slipped in wicks of cotton and lit them and we washed like that, illuminated.

Shimmery from my sea voyage, will I be recognizable to my cousin? Or will she scream, slam the door in my face, and resume her life as a citizen, a computer programmer, though she is younger than me and pregnant with her second child, or so I heard?

LALOO'S GUIDE TO HITCHHIKING

Perhaps you are already reading this in the bus station of Columbus, Ohio, and maybe a Thai monk, complete with saffron robes and a washcloth, has just run off with your last seventy bucks. You gave him your change purse to go get ice cream for you, him, and the family of eleven Mennonite children en route to Buffalo, New York. He didn't come back and now you're stuck. May I suggest hitchhiking as a convenient way to reunite with your family and friends in Oregon or some other place. There are ten basic rules upon which this informative manual is based. In each section, I will address one of these rules, although you can refer to the "Rough notes for conduct page" at any time as a quick reference.

Rough Notes for Conduct Page

THE TEN ESSENTIAL RULES
OF HITCHHIKING

1 Keep a notebook.
2 Accept things as they come without making the minor, necessary effort to change them.
3 When you are sleepy, tired, and desperate, do not ask, "What can I do?"

4   When you get in the car and you feel you have made a mistake, do not breathe deeply. Murderers can smell fear on your breath. Rapists, for example, pace themselves to your panic.

5   Say everything is stupid and magnificent.

6   Divorce then re-marry the road at least twice.

7   Go farther each time.

8   Sometimes, stand outside the house where your family members are drinking their candlelit broth, and breathe it in, the atmosphere of barbeque, TV, and childhood, then walk back to the highway from that position.

9   If you must drink water, pee standing up. Carry tubing and/or disposable cones for this purpose, especially if you're a woman.

10   Lie through your teeth and accept cigarettes, even if you just slide them behind your ear like James Dean. In general pretend to be tougher than your father, blanker and crazier than your mother with her particular interests and phobias. Insist upon the window opened a crack. Write down what you see until you feel sick. They'll stop. They don't want you to puke all over the dash. That's when you get out and wait for a different ride. Number ten is huge. Your survival as a hitchhiker depends upon it. I love you; please don't die.

1. KEEP A NOTEBOOK

I wanted to go and did. All hitchhiking is related to mating. Is it mating to disperse your body as a referent? The woman in a body, a person standing at the edge of the road, always refers to her complex choice to go. Is it normal and beautiful to hitchhike? Is it working-class? Perhaps it is useful to point out that one in every three hitchhikers is a murderer, like the man with the empty oil can at the side of the road. "That's too bad you ran out of gas." "Oh, I didn't. Just didn't think anyone would stop, just a man by himself, so I held up the can."

Also, never forget that passengers and drivers are interchangeable in this culture. Even a driver, for example, can experience days that fail, like air conditioning, despite the integrity of the actual body. A driver can find himself adrift on the map. However, as a hitchhiker, you are certainly vulnerable to . . . I don't want to scare you. Just think of a set of teeth from a body next to the body. The same body! Like that. You want to avoid this sort of thing as much as possible. Check the eyes of the driver before you get in, for signs of redness. He may look normal but you don't know what he's got beneath the seat.

Once again, my name is Laloo. It means red. This is point one of my ten red points. I am not a very good writer but I do not feel you have made a mistake in reading/purchasing this guide to the thoroughfares of your massive nation. I'm sure you must have heard the myth of the hitchhiker whose heart was found next to her body, wrapped in a T-shirt. On the positive side, maybe ... maybe it is amazing what happens. Maybe it's George Clooney slowing down in a Subura Impreza, here in Nebraska, to film his next movie, "A Hitchhiker's Guide to Nebraska." Are you so beautiful? Does George choose you at random from a sea of potential hitchhikers? Maybe he will invite you to his villa on Lake Como and get you a job with his people. Maybe he will fall in love with you and they will make TV of that, complete with Parminder Nagra, the star of *Bend It Like Beckham*, cast as you. Are you British and did you grow up watching your mother iron your father's turban fabric, spritzing it with starch water? Or maybe you are the driver, though this is technically not an example of hitchhiking, and George Clooney gets in, in character. This is switching. It is completely new sexual territory: not for everyone, but for you.

Why are you hitchhiking? It is crazy. Please keep a notebook or log of some kind open on your lap. Describe the weather. It is difficult to write slowly at speeds but not even I, a highly experienced, slightly blemished girl who thrives on hazard, can stop you from going if you have gone. If you're reading this, for example, then I can guarantee that your father is grinding the whisky in his jaw before swallowing it and you are taking steps to leave your house with its faux marble countertop. Cars slow down. You are looking at the cars to see what they mean. Good girl.

A car slows down. I have neither a gun nor a spoon nor a syringe. This is the dream of hitchhiking: a passivity to fate, yet an acuity. There on the verge. In England and Scotland, it is a verge of boiled tar, cat's eyes, and Lady Anne's lace. In your country, I mean this one: are you a girl? Are you half dead after a complicated journey? You tell me what you see, there at the rim of the highway asphalt. It's always purple next to yellow in the handbook of roadside flora. In contrast to this pastoral scene, a hitchhiker resembles a monster in a cartoon. She is invariably a dingy figure against a globular background with purple and yellow furnishings such as curtains. I saw this on Scooby Doo and also Hong Kong Phooey, in a motel room in Utah.

A vagary of coloring is monstrous. Passing through or hesitating, considering the purchase of a coffee malted in a sit-down restaurant such as Perkins, you will always be distinct from the local vegetation. For example, I once hitchhiked from Atlanta to Boston in a Brazilian red dress over jeans. Having misjudged the heat, I reddened then darkened further. Dark red, I stood in the sun. Light-headed, I got in. "I'll turn on the AC once we get going."

Okay. In addition to keeping a notebook, I suggest you purchase some Levi's and take a bath in them, prior to your departure for the open road, to ensure that they conform to your shape whatever the weather; this reduces friction, if you have to run.

2. ACCEPT THINGS AS THEY COME WITHOUT MAKING THE MINOR, NECESSARY EFFORT TO CHANGE THEM

Dogs not coolers. There in the bed of the truck like Jim-bob hitchhiking back to Walton's mountain after his long day at the lumberyard just outside of town. In Punjab, there is no such thing as a hitchhiker exactly—there's just a girl, for example, dangling her legs from the back of a tonga (a bullock cart with horns), watching a landscape of citrine rape blossoms go by. It was me and now it is an addiction to citrus codes, squares and triangles of yellow encountered elsewhere in life, as marking a path, the right way to go/continue, which is difficult to know for sure, hitchhiking, there in the fabulous world that values correctness above sorrow. It might mean sorrow if you rely on an inner sense of fortune (signs and aspects) to proceed upon a thoroughfare, but that is better than certain death at the hands of a murderer, who disguises his intention with bags of groceries on the backseat.

I will talk you through an example with a car in it. Imagine a black Saab pulls up, complete with a driver in a pink shirt and three bags of groceries on the passenger seat. "Oh, let me just put all this in the back. I won't be a moment. Do you want me to put your backpack in the trunk?" Fine. This could go either way. The pink, in this example, is good but I propose to you that it is the Saab that is suspect. Not the Saab per se. No, it's the Saab. Avoid Saabs. They have a reputation for poor mechanical whateverness and so it will always sound feasible when the driver complains that the engine doesn't sound right. Then it becomes difficult for you, there in the car, on the verge, when the driver gets out to pop the hood. "I'll just be a minute." Right. No. No, no, no. It is fatal to wait in the car. My advice to you is to accept things as they are, i.e., the reality of the situation, and to get out of the Saab immediately. To go is to accept. Accept and get. Get out of the car. "Get out of the car, Laloo." I once heard a voice say that exact same thing to me as what I am saying to you, and look at me. I survived. To summarize: Pink not red. Red not yellow. You can purchase flash cards to accompany this guide from any local bookseller of good repute. I will make them then you buy them, okay?

3. WHEN YOU ARE SLEEPY, TIRED, AND DESPERATE, DO NOT ASK "WHAT CAN I DO?"

Like a raccoon in the headlights. Like deer who falter midleap across the barrier separating traffic. Like the glossy, nocturnal animals with their two children in tow, like human mothers. Like a person at the end of a marriage who, homeless in her or his home, walks as if without direction towards the highway. Like a trucker reaching for speed. Like an irreversible experience of genesis, which is childbirth, whether it takes place in a hospital or not: "Honey!" "Honey, can you hear me? Honey, open your eyes. If you can't push her out in the next twenty minutes, we're gonna have to cut you open."

I am writing this from my housing unit, in the life or space after hitchhiking but I can assure you that my memories of fingers are as fresh as ever. Fingers is not the right word. I mean, what happens, if you don't snap to attention when the car slows down or speeds up erratically. I do not know if I am living here illegally but the effort involved in getting back on the road is in many ways thoroughly appalling, like eggs with ketchup.

No, I like ketchup. Something else. Mayonnaise. I need to send off a form to interface with the Department of Homeland Security, updating my address, but when I download the form, Form 93 a, I discover that it is illegal not to report a change of address and that one (Laloo) has a three-month grace period in which to do so. It has been a year or so since I hung up my hat and so I am nervous. I write this guide out of nervousness but also conviction. Conviction is not the word. I mean gratitude. No, something else. Mayonnaise. A way to make things palatable, whether you are at home or abroad, like the moon. That is from an Imagist poem I learned to recite by heart as a schoolgirl in England. Here

in the heartland, I stunt the line but do not ask, "What can I do?"
I focus instead upon memories and outcomes, fingers and cars. I
don't know what happened to you. I'm sorry about it but I can't
stop now and neither can you. Repeat after me the words of Frida
Kahlo, from the wheelchair diary she kept as a young woman:
EVERYTHING IS STUPID AND MAGNIFICENT.

4. DON'T PANIC

There in Yellowstone, picking your way along a boardwalk be-
tween the creamy blue explosions, or there in Manhattan, drink-
ing your coffee on the steps opposite Caffe Reggio. Zigzagging
across the country, extend your hand in gratitude for the free
baguette but do not meet the baker later for a dip in a river, even
if it seems powerful to you, the way he extends his floury, meaty
hand. Avoid men. This is not the time to be involved with men in
any capacity, even on a perverted/inspiring uncle-and-niece-type
basis. You don't need an uncle. You need the ocean. I think this is
what hitchhiking is primarily about. It is about the sea, which is
ocean, and the dark corner with the tiny unstable table at which
you sit, looking down at the pink waves. Perhaps you are finally
at Big Sur, crushing a capsule of orange powder onto the table-
cloth. I don't know what that is, but I see it. I see your intensity. If
I can see it, then others can too, so you want to keep your wits
about you and wait until morning before you head down to the

beach. It's all ahead of you, crossing the street to the parking lot and then the beach. It is arrival in reverse to approach an ocean. Are you an immigrant? Don't panic, immigrant. There are places to curl up in under a cliff, in a cave, and in the morning you will be covered with starfish opening and closing all over your body. Encrusted, riveted, bright orange, what will you do? What will you do with your new body? What will you make it do? I made it stop but that was a decision. Beatrice, Nebraska, glowed a deep green from the highway. I said stop and they stopped and they were angry and I walked across fields to get there, the Beatrice downtown. Keep walking, Laloo, is what I said to myself in my exhausted state, and that is what I say to you, as a way of guiding you through your life which is aberrant. One season, you got itchy feet glancing up from the conveyor belt at the high window where the weather and the night sky were. Am I right? Inside every hitchhiker is a memory of home or factory that haunts him. Her. The spectral figure at the highway exit, all bones and a red T-shirt in the ruby-red taillights. It is a car. I said stop and it stopped, but don't get in. I am writing this guide exclusively for you.

RULES 5 TO 10

You write them. Choose your preferences. Perhaps you hate the ocean. Perhaps you wear a crucifix inside your transparent blouse. Perhaps you are a U.S. citizen on a sort of holiday. Perhaps you have a destination, such as Houston, in mind at all hours. Perhaps you have a gun. Perhaps you are a man. Perhaps you are red not green, I mean green not red. Perhaps you are a driver and are interested in the psychology of hitchhikers though not in being one yourself. No, you are a hitchhiker in all likelihood. I write to you, hopefully, in the zigzag, reaching you there. My address is 786 Thomas Street, Beatrice, NE, 80349. My name is Laloo. Please write to me, from the border of Texas and Mexico, where the candlelit vigils are held each Day of the Dead for the dead who died when crossing. Light a candle for me when you get there on your grand loop. I invite you to write the remaining rules for the people who keep going. I couldn't. I had to stop. "She came too far." Someone said those words about a Cambodian cat that was brought to New York on an airplane, by a refugee worker. This cat attacked the other cats in the person's apartment so that the person had to come home each day and rotate the cats from room to room. Like that cat, I could not do it beyond a certain point: be real. You are real in the day. When you write about the future from a place of white crosses entwined with bougainvillea and plastic roses, or when you nestle the candle in the wet sand next to the dangerous river, I will read your beautiful words. "Prepare to travel, tie the pack. Open the flag." Perhaps I should meet you there, at the edge of the edge, but I cannot go farther south or west than this.

NOTES TO STOP

THE CAR (A—L)

Floral. I eat oysters. This is obvious. Hello New Mexico, hello Arizona, hello San Diego. Can I have a cup of coffee and a plate of twelve? There's a painting on the wall of the restaurant: Red Canna. On a red background, it's as if she's painted the bones of a human _____. This is it, excised. Suspended. I came to this country to say: "Lasagna." "This is my pink book." "This is my red book." "Licking books, boys and girls get thirsty."

Hitchhiking, you tolerate the gun edging up your skirt or pointed to your head, as if to say, take off your jeans. It's 2005. Take off your jeans now. Bunched up around my ankles, the jeans are concrete or might as well be, ankle-deep. Eastern Standard Time. Mountain Time. The car is moving at such monstrous speeds, fatally subtracting a continent. 863, 36. Trees and landscapes. Why not? Each thing that happens is too much now.

B.

A woman with grey crispy hair looks up from her knitting. The car slows and I, convulsing like a mermaid back into my jeans, which are wet, look the driver in the eye, daring him to accelerate/defy the laws of a small town, and casually open the door.

Damaged goods opens the door with her little finger; where am I? Where is this? 011 44 1895 673537. My father answers the phone. In the booth, I stand tall and proud as I shout: "Everything's fine, Daddy." I like English. "Do you need money?" He knows. As a young man, he hitchhiked from Greece to Calais, his money knotted in a handkerchief deep in a battered blue attaché. Did he drink beer? "I could have married a German woman." What kind of sex did my father have in Frankfurt? I imagine that he enjoyed it very much but that it could not compete with a history of violence, a heritage of wings: the flutter and blur of muscles and knives. What made him leave his country at nighttime, unprepared financially for the long journey ahead? As a child, massaging his legs with mustard seed oil—what is a girl?—I was able to fit a finger into the silver dent on his thigh. His right leg. "Don't stop!"

c.

I am writing to you.

d.

The woman with the grey body knotting blue yarn just stares, her item mystically stagnant in her lap, on the verge of becoming a

dress, a cap, booties. "Good afternoon," I say to her—"GOOD AF-
TERNOON"—louder and louder until she looks down, resuming
her work.

A monster is always itinerant. She has a suitcase not a shopping
cart; is brown not pink. What happens to the color pink when it's
left out in a dish? Shrimp. Fish from the sea but also from rivers.
That's what he said to her as he slid out his Colt 45: "I smell fish."
It was a bad moment but she made eye contact. This is something
she learned as a child on the dark days when her father dowsed
her with scotch then lit a cigarette for emphasis. Was it a dark day
or was it acculturation? Was it survival? Was it useful? Did it help
her to become a more successful monster when her time came to
emigrate?

Then I took my spot. Extended my thumb. Tried to catch the at-
tention of female drivers/passengers. "Nephrite, flint, lava, slag."
"Slag, flint, nephrite." I said these things deep inside me to keep
still, a recipient, part of the great streaming that carries others to
their destinations. "My life as a woman." I've read about this in
books and seen it in films. "Why are you here? Why are you say-
ing these things to me?"—Nicholas Cage. "Why are you saying
these things to ME?"—Cher. Then he kicks over the table, scoops
her up in his arms and hauls her out of the kitchen like a tray of
unbaked scones. "Take the skin from my bones." "Until there's
nothing left."

E .

Laloo, get out of the car. This is a voice in the head, a palm on the cruising bones. Perhaps he bites her as she panics, fumbling for the door. Cars whizzing by in a frenzy of rubies and diamonds. And spits. "Know what? You have really ugly eyebrows." Right. Absolutely fabulous. Thanks so much. (Routed. If not okay then sent: propelled by invisible forces. She says, "what?") The car door slams, to her left. What? It's raining. Someone yells from a passing car: "Go back to Mexico!" Laloo backs off the highway and into the trees.

F .

I am writing to you, as always. This is the story about a girl who went too far. There were consequences, but I like to think of her, the girl who left hearth and home, as re-established in a town or city central to your country, washing dishes like a robot or falling in love with a needy, cool robot.

G .

Laloo get out of the car now. (Beatrice, Nebraska. A mall just outside of Eugene, a bus ride into town. Boulder with its black mirrors in the hills above construction. By mirrors I mean irons, an upsurge in the plates. A sort of, geographically, stop it Laloo. Hold it right there.) Get out of the car in the west, pre-West, where the four directions are more vividly displayed than in, for example, Maine or the boundary waters or the Black Hills. I don't know what you're doing, there in the spotless rental like a dreaming artist. Green, green, red. The red of the landscape, west of Kansas, is the opposite of the silvers and greys she was bred on, in the United Kingdom. Each morning it rained and now, she is travel-ing smoothly across a plateau of sunlight, counting colors. It seems to Laloo—does it?—that she's been removed from a place (northwest London) with great force.

H.

Are you red? Did you read books on a windowsill all morning like a Bronte heroine, hidden by a curtain but extending a foot every few minutes to the radiator? Did the rain batter the windowpane and was it a day off from the logic of childhood? As a child, did you believe in the voice in your head, the hand on your bones? Did you feel safe beneath the covers in your pink pajamas? Of course you did. But are you red now? Are you red forever, from your hazardous travels that brought you to a different place? Or was it easy? Was it incremental? Were you a girl then a woman, a boy then a man? Did you grow wings when you were a cat, and fly away to a different but no less lucrative scene, complete with mice and milk and massage therapy for animals?

Get out of the car at the next stoplight. This is a town. It is a pop-
ulation of souls and so, you'll be safe here. Though you are clearly
damaged from your travels, this is nothing that a Christian econ-
omy, with its emphasis upon recovery and the provisions to be
made, can't accommodate. Indeed, there are classes at the local
Presbyterian church, on Jefferson and Fourth, each Wednesday
night, for those seeking to make a permanent home in this coun-
try or part of a country. One is taught how to open cans, I've
heard. Not you. Others. People who traveled even farther to get
here and for different reasons. This will all become apparent in
the special meeting dedicated to the future, a kind of workshop
for incoming, needy, slightly monstrous-looking beings in need
of a hair wash. "Let's build a future together," says the greeter's T-
shirt. Behind him, there is a banner, balloons, coffee, a group of
five people drinking coffee—clearly, these are the beings—and a
promise of shelter. Once everyone is settled, the greeter goes from
person to person handing out coupons for a free week's stay at
The Angel House, a hostel for those in need of home and love.
If you want this, if you want the support of a community, then
get out of the car and go to the nearest good-looking church and
kneel. These people are good. They won't ask you for your ID.
They are often elderly and may have lost a parent, an animal, a
husband, or a wife. They believe in strangers and they believe in

you, though you clearly have medical problems what with the hard, reddened patches all over your face and arms. "Do you speak Eng-lish?" "Are you allergic to cats?" I think the greeter is offering you a place in his own home, in exchange for light help with daily chores. Here, you are on your own. I can get you out of the car but I cannot do more than this. You are darkness in a dress. You are kneeling in a church and opening your mouth for the delicate paper that dissolves on your tongue.

Assimilation is a technology of growth.

J.

"Can I get you another cup of coffee? Oh lord, Angie! Angie, get over here! Somebody, dial 911! Oh, honey, are you okay? Oh, hi... no, we don't need an ambulance. She's coming to. Honey? Honey, can you hear me?" But here comes the ambulance anyway, with its mission of retrieval, its complex medicines for the traumas experienced even in passing.

K.

Laloo gets out of the car and takes five steps before collapsing. She descends in a reverie, waking up: a) in the trunk of a car, bound at the wrists, b) in Beatrice, Nebraska, where her loss of memory permits her to embark upon a small town life complete with under-the-table employment at the local diner and an amorous line cook who lifts up his T-shirt and apron to show her where he was stabbed as a child in Tijuana, c) in a few moments, gathering her strength to stand and head away from the highway into the trees.

L.

L is for Laloo, darkness in a dress. Her body is very vulnerable tonight, there in the forest next to the highway. Only children on road trips notice her and wave. In her red dress, she is like a girl in a fairytale, geographically. (All the branches behind her have begun to stir.) This is what a girl does in stories: she walks slowly, almost meditatively, along the perimeter of a forest and then she veers. Are there forests in London? Yes. Are there forests in the ocean? Yes. Are there forests in New Jersey and Nebraska? Yes. She finds each forest in turn and enters it as a test of desire. It is radical desire but, unable to stop feeling what she came there to feel, she can't stop and now she is in the thick part of the country stumbling over the roots. This is walking—technically, no longer hitchhiking but something else. An intensive travel. Is this a forest or is it just a stand of pines next to the highway? Is it regrowth? Is it a tree or trees? Yes. A red girl goes into this yes and is never seen again, which will break the hearts of her parents when they receive the shoe. It is always a shoe on the asphalt, recovered from the scene then wrapped in paper and placed in a ziplock bag. Is this a scene? L is for Laloo kicking off her shoes and breathing deeply from her toes to her head, allaying her deep fear of the gathering dark. Is it dark yet? Yes. Quite dark. I can't see her anymore—just a shiver, moving through the trees. Something is coming towards her in the moment of contact that precedes alteration, something huge, but I can't see what it is. The question of home dissolves into the question of trees. L is for love which is blood: the gathering speed of a pulse though the person is standing very still in the space before touch there in the darkness which is real.

ACKNOWLEDGMENTS

Sections of this work previously appeared in *Chain* #7 and as the chapbook *Autobiography of a Cyborg*, published by Leroy in 2000.

I would like to extend my gratitude to my students at Naropa University, in the Fall 2005 writing class "Evolution and Mutation," for the beautiful conversations about narrative as sites of pre-conception; Andrea Spain for sharing her thinking on evolution within populations; Gina McGovern for painting the alcove red, orange, and gold; and Rohini Kapil for her phrase, "The future of color."

I would like to thank Laura Mullen for making me re-think cyborgs and thank you, also, to Thelonious Rider for asking, "Mama, who was the first person who was ever born?" which made me think for the first time of the connection between a monster and a citizen. In particular, I thank Leon Works for making a space for writing, in which writing feels possible again.

LEON WORKS A PRESS FOR EXPERIMENTAL PROSE AND

THE "THINKING TEXT" PUBLISHER: *Renee Gladman* PROOFREADER: *Rachel Bernstein*

Leon wishes to extend a deep bow to Melissa Buzzeo for her uncountable assistance on this project; belated thanks to Gloria Frym, Claudia Rankine, and Laird Hunt for their support during last year's fundraising efforts; and lastly, much love and appreciation to Mei-mei Berssenbrugge for her support.